LITTLE LETTERS ON THE SKIN

A partnership between the Cleave: Bay Area Women Writers
Reading Series and The Liminal Center

LITTLE LETTERS ON THE SKIN

A partnership between the Cleave: Bay Area Women Writers
Reading Series and The Liminal Center

Edited by Raina J. León

Cleave Press
2017

First Printing: 2017

ISBN 978-0-9990266-0-1

Cleave: Bay Area Women Writers

https://www.facebook.com/cleavereadingseries/?ref=br_rs

Ordering Information:
Special discounts are available on quantity purchases by corporations, associations, educators, and others. For details, contact the publisher at the above listed address.

U.S. trade bookstores and wholesalers: Please contact Cleave Press Tel (925) 322-3427; cleavebayarea@gmail.com

Table of Contents

What Being a Part of the Liminal Community in Oakland Means to Me by Heather Schubert

I am a survivor of childhood sexual abuse, physical abuse, kidnapping, domestic violence and rape. As a direct result of the abuse I suffered I now have several physical disabilities and limitations that inhibit my ability to support myself and my children as a single mother. Creative outlets such as writing and art have aided me greatly in my healing processes over the years, so I know firsthand how important community projects that support the arts can be.

The primary purpose of the leaders of a free country is to insure that all things are possible for all people regardless of gender, race, ethnicity, sexual preference or social and economic status. It certainly should be the charge of every human being on this planet to turn this into a global norm. The list of people who take on this charge is a short one. Gina Goldblat is one of those people and she has done a great service in opening an amazing writing center in Oakland CA called The Liminal.

Liminal helps to address the issues of gender disparity in the field of writing, publishing and the reviewing of published material. There will be a need for places like Liminal until gone are the days in which women question their power, their influence, their voice and most of all their worth. Having a place in which we can come together to write strengthens our common well-being and pushes us forward as a group.

It's true that we live in a better world than our mothers and grandmothers, but what are we leaving for our daughters and granddaughters? Empowering the people within the community is paramount to breaking the cycle of sexism, racism and gentrification in Oakland and everywhere. It is also a key part of dismantling the cycle of violence and discrimination. Protecting women is not the answer to ending violence against them. Education, empowerment and body equality are the building blocks to the foundation of a world without violence against women. While Liminal is a feminist, womanist, writing center its doors are open to everyone and the programs offered there encourage people from all genders, races and walks of life to collaborate together. It is this type of solidarity that will help to build a brighter and safer tomorrow for future generations and start us down the path of discovering exactly how to make all things possible for all people.

I stopped writing and creating art ten years ago after I was raped again. Participating as a Writer in Residence, teaching classes and attending events at Liminal has allowed me to tap into my own personal creativity once more. I have begun publishing again and I had my first art show. I've experienced a boatload of support and learned how to promote myself and my talents. I'm a part of the grant writing committee and one of my personal goals is to help offer free or low cost programs to the children who live in the immediate area. Being a part of Liminal might just be the most important thing I do in my lifetime. I guess you could say, it means a great deal to me.

Wound Tight

All tied up in knots
A yarn ball of raw emotions
Wound tight
Spun strong
Cork stopped
Waiting to burst
Erupt in a single fashion
Of colors and dye lots
Shades of blues and greens
Spilling emotions
Onto the blank pages of my mind
I dip my brush into those watery hues
And glide free.

The Goddess In Me

I don't wanna be anyone's Isis or Hera,
My Goddess is a Whore!
No room for virgins or bores.
I'm raw and I'm blunt
No seal of approval needed,
Artimis on the hunt.
Feels too good to get what I want.
You might find a little Venus
Between us.
But just enough to make you sad
When I'm gone before daybreak.
Guess you weren't really the best I'd ever had.
Sure, I'll call, text or tweet.
Na, really it's swipe to the right or delete.
Five minute immortals
No time to deceive.
Temptation's a bitch
Just ask the infamous Eve.
Aphrodite, Goddess of love?
Maybe....
But more like untamed sensuality.
Fantasies are a waste
Come n get you a real taste.
Kali devours you whole.
When I'm done, I'm done.
I don't care if you come.
Today you've fed MY soul.
I don't believe in shame.
Yea, baby to me you're just a game.
And you'll be lucky if I remember your name.
Don't ask me what color your eyes are
That's taking it a little too far.
No matter how Godlike you seem,

I'll never trip over you and fall.
Face it, boy toy,
You're just one divine booty call!

Those were the days
When someone close died,
either in the hospital or at home,
we cooked. How many times
did I arrive home from school to find a note
on the kitchen counter:
Jack Roseman died. Go to the store
and buy six fryers. Season them well and
bake them at 400.
Bring them
to the Roseman's. You know
where they live. I'll meet you there,
or
Rose Jackman died today.
In the freezer you'll find
a brisket, cooked last week. Thaw it.
I'll pick you up at five. We'll heat it
at the Jackman's. Poor Barry!
Today, if I were 16 again,
There would be
a text message, the same
instructions. My mother,
long gone now, knew
how to cook for comfort,
how to arrive, arms full
of sustenance, exactly
when all seemed lost.

What Scattered in the Wind by Rebecca Gomez Farrell

Hollow rasps of laughter pestered her to wakefulness. Any noise would have done the same, though she clamped her eyelids together in protest. For years, Ruth had heard nothing but the teakettle's hiss or the slow scrape of her cane against the camper's floor panels. The creaking sound of her voice rarely interrupted the silence. Unlike the other wayfarers, Ruth had never developed the habit of talking to herself. She didn't care to hear what she'd have to say.

"Hee-hee, hee-he-heee!"

Ruth plugged her ears, but it did no good, the laughter too sharp, too loud. Too out of place in this canyon between unnamed mesas. She drew the powder-blue afghan around her shoulders, a shell pattern she'd crocheted the last winter. In a few more months, she'd burn it on the grill, watch through narrowed eyes as embers chased each thread. It was a way to mark seasons in a place without trees, to remind herself that the world cycled on and she took up space within it.

"Hee-he-hee, hee!"

Her eyes fluttered open. She toyed with pretending at sleep for a moment longer, but that wouldn't do -- Ruth had never shirked from what life threw in her path, except that once, so long ago she could not say when it might have been.

Slats of light sheared through the blinds. She shrugged the blanket off, rose in an ivory-colored slip. A yellowed knit shawl remained on a hook by the stove, one of its unraveled threads hanging low enough to catch flame. Breath caught in her ribcage at the sight of it. Once, a man in a blue, a shield on his chest, had asked her questions of it, and she'd feigned absentmindedness, that she knew. Now, she could not recall the circumstances.

She opened the door.

The RV groaned as her weight shifted off the last metal step, sun-blindness taking a minute to blink away. Another trailer had pulled in down by the trickle of a stream. A fresh coat of red dust rose two feet up its exterior. Raised letters spelled *Chieftain* on its side, the same model as Ruth's rusty old boat. Beyond it, a child ran in wild circles, stopping for tickles from a mother whose lawn chair sat close to the sun-cracked ground.

Scratchy with disuse, Ruth's voice sounded as painful to her ears as the boy's laughter. "Where'd you come from?"

His bouncy black curls fell still as his head followed her vibration. Where eye sockets once had been, vacant crevices sizzled with licks of flame.

Ruth swallowed her gasp of recognition with a scowl. It had been so many years, enough to baste and rend the veil of age again, to twist lies into the truths she'd told herself.

The mother rose. A bright white shawl fell from her shoulders, crumbling to ashes in the wind. The boy reached for her hand, and the two visitors melded together, flesh fusing to sticky flesh.

Ruth recognized the mirth lines she'd once worn on the mother's face, the freckles on her nose. They marked skin that dissolved as mother and child advanced, sparking dust devils of detritus that danced to the desert floor. A different question came to Ruth's lips, the one she'd had no answer for when all this had begun. "Why'd you come?"

"We've always been here," said the mother. "You've just forgotten."

Ruth spat at the ground. "No, no. I just wish you'd never been."

Enflamed tissue uncoupled from the child's arm like black grains from white in a flipped sandscape. Smoke brought tears to Ruth's eyes, but she held her ground, even as the child's searing grasp brought the familiar sickly stench of her torment.

Ruth had never shirked from what life threw in her path. Except that once. Except that once.

END

SnakeMOM

Hardly more than ever. My mother slips on the snake skin in the hallway at night. In our childhood hallway she slithers like a thing without feet. How does a snake climb stairs? Does a snake climbing stairs look more like an escalator? In the green grass of New York Springtime it is soft and dewy and cushiony for the behind. When I got outside in California and placed my tush on the ground, I felt spiny and prickly and water deprived and I got up quickly, as if I had sat on a flame. What the fuck is wrong with this grass? This was my introduction to the California that is, when I was coming to the California I'd heard of. No one talks about how you will miss things that are lush. Or that you will crave the brown water that drips off the hotdogs from the New York stands, because somehow those stands make it acceptable to eat hot dogs, even though you fucking know full well what is in hot togs. You will just walk and walk and walk until you get from one tippy top of the island to the bowery bottom and further and go straight on walking over the Brooklyn Bridge into Dumbo and past all the things you can't afford to even pick up for fear of dropping and breaking them and not being able to buy them and on to a free box of books that will make you late for work when you stop under the bridge to rifle through them and take what your arms can carry and quickwalk lately to work with them and say look guys, i found these, but I'm sorry I'm late, it's just there were free books. Snakes don't read books so my mother has to come back to her form that has fingers to sit at the blue dining picnic table and take a century to finish one paperback in two minute increments. Though some days she lights a scented candle, opens the window, hours before my father will be home, and says fuck it to the vacuum, the mop, the ringing phone. She says fuck it to the piss on the walls of the bathrooms because the boy children don't aim or aim for the walls or because somehow my father thinks it's excusable to miss or that it is part of a man's right to get some on the bowl. She says fuck it to the unmade bed, to the car in the driveway ready to run errands, to the cheese that was eaten in a sitting and was suppose to be for a week of lunches but now needs to be replaced. She says fuck it to the chicken nuggets in the fridge still frozen, she says happily, there is dog hair on every surface, there are boogers on the boy's bedroom wall, there are ladybugs in the damned windowsills and fuck it and I will read and she reads How Stella Got Her Groove Back and she is not a snake and the world outside has soft grass and likes bottoms and it is hardly more than ever that she does this fuckit thing with herself but right now she is doing it and she would take a hotdog if one appeared to take then wouldn't she.

Dogma and Natural Symbols*

When I sit down
it doesn't come on like it does
when I lay out like a horizon
on the rumpled, pre-sweat-soaked sheets
that hold the whole living past in
*the lower stories of the skyscraper**
is the truth
told in gasps
over the wreckage of two towers brought down
of two bodies brought together and taken down by each other,
by need
Just give me New York where it was simple
The catcallingbeautiful call-you-by-the-end-of-the-day-parts-
of-Manhattan where the Dominicans licked their lips from behind
the brims of their hats
and the heat was thick on their brows
and it was easy
To think about going to bed and not doing it
Expansive
                        Vulgar
the type of classless we don't let on   we embody
in the crowds of literati we run with
until the bookstores doors have shut behind us
the 40's clinked true
the stronghold of a strange configuration of
tongue and heterofelixble and dildo and the cat under the chair
Let me be loud as you were before I had you fixed.
Before I pissed off the dumpster diving crustpunk that lived
with 3 men in his bedroom and complained that I never wanted to
come over; who only liked my cat when her *instincts got the better*
of her *and attacked him at times in uncontrollable outbursts.* * I just
didn't want sex beneath a bed, on a mound, to the soundtrack and
smellscape of sweatstocks and groundcreak and don't let my skin

---

touch anything but your skin. One fled to the forest to find himself. Others hung on to the fringe of civilized, grilled skunk in the backyard, and alienated their black neighbors in the front; bringing their showy ambivalence, their shiny madness, and stankheart to the midst of history repeating itself over the skin color of the **West Oakland** neighborhood. Burner vehicles: the fucked up throwbacks to childhood that white kids gone grown up will do for kicks and because they never were able to give up the nipple.

as a toddler

my pointer finger outstretched

awaits the gel

to rub on my gums
for the lack of sensation it evokes
the spirit of addiction
rampant in my blood
they both worried they'd give me
and both blamed the other for
the pressure heightens
full with the most of what it has to spew
gentle, rocking notions, mocking a silent selfperception
the shamesolitude spastic hands
making a multitude of my need
ache from a jawbone parted
after years of clenching down
heartache confirmed
a checkmarkedbox bartered with
Stoneset pupils and pubic bones incessantly probing the air
to find the nooks of each other they could rest in
Two blank spaces
Goggles worn to see better
and fogged over in the spatial refractions of the sun underwater

green algae bloom on the nails of a lover
Behind the molars
where the waxy imprint lay
Me down
I once thought this was an act of giving
*Found Text from *Psychology and Religion* by Carl Gustav Jung

38th Avenue

When the white man says its time to cross the street, you may safely place you right foot from the sidewalk onto the pavement below, followed by your left and make your way to the other side.

If there is no white man walking at your corner, you are shit out of luck.

Here, there is street parking. When we park, we put our blinkers on, parallel park against the curb, wait until the traffic stops to get out. The shoulder is only large enough to carefully place your car out of the way. An inch or two off and you may find your mirror smashed off in the morning.

Our lives are worth less, so we don't have space to exit our vehicles safely.

On Piedmont Avenue, there is room for several large bodies, plenty of room to swing open the driver's door without even looking and climb out, pay the meter, go get a bubble tea.

In this place where someone hacks off the tree branches outside my building in the nighttime, a trio of folks drag a dryer into the street and ties it to the top of their truck on a Tuesday after midnight, I worry that the teenagers are crossing the street at a bend in the road and giggling instead of looking both ways, not that they just bought some pot from the neighbors- that's what teenagers will do.

Just because the happy hours take place below my window and the preferred beverages are forties.

The neighborhood watch is out to profile, criticize, uproot the real life.

Through the heavy doors I listen to my critics. "She claims it is a feminist space, yet she is hosting a fashion blogging event. How Ironic. Google her. Hmm, calling this the Laurel." The man's busy fingers on his smart phone, I can see their white skin, their blond hair, the extra they carry around the middle, to hold the judgment they have of me. "We are like spies," says the man. They fiddle with my mail slot.

As they are walking to the car, I open the door; nonchalantly attend to a cardboard box on the sidewalk. She returns, "Oh yes, we are sorry to have missed the event. Just heard about it afterwards and were checking out the space."

Sure. Hello the face of judgment. The faces. The lies. I heard you, playing self-elected investigator. Good fucking afternoon.

I didn't know I had a smell until my body turned into a cannibal. Little girls and little boys smell the same—even down there— like apple juice, or the innocence of the skin on an upper lip. The difference came on me with pubic hair, a need for Secret antiperspirant, and the used pads I lifted up to my face still warm, thinking about raw steak slapped on the counter.

I get why it scares them. Why they have to make jokes about it—the story of the blind man at the fish market—but they don't have their faces close enough if they think that.

Meat is dangerous. It doesn't decompose like vegetable matter. You can't compost with it. It used to have a heartbeat.

There is something to it—the smell. The messiness of it— stewing in a pair of tights, locked under panties made of cheap synthetic fabric. After a day of sweating when I cross and uncross my legs compulsively, wondering how strong it is. How obvious.

Of course men have their own smell, especially the ones I like. There is a certain unmistakable mix of dirty hair and unwashed jeans that sets my nose twitching and my pulse thumping. JS is a member of this tribe—dirt under his fingernails, black Levis, and hair defiantly greasy. He isn't very cute, but he makes up for it with snottiness.

"I like the way you ladies smell."

He exclaims. He's holding forth in a battered kitchen, the epicenter of a ramshackle Friday night party.

"I don't mean perfume neither."

His mouth is in a half-smirk, as usual, but his tone is serious in its admiration.

"I mean after a couple of days without a shower."

The vodka has long since erased any traces of my own self-consciousness about this line of conversation—and taken most of my common sense with it. I just can't resist.

"I worry about it sometimes."

I bite my lip, making my best doe eyes.

Locking a gaze in like fingers on a forearm.

"Like before I left the house today, when I was putting on my leggings?"

I pause for effect. I'm getting to him.

"I noticed I smelled different."

Breathy. Marilyn Monroe innocence.

"I think it depends on where I am, you know, in my cycle."

I can't stop myself. Staring deep—seeing the waves of it breaking over his head. Whispering in his ear.

"I have to go now." He says matter of fact, reaching for his smokes, not breaking eye contact.

"Why?" I ask. He looks defiant, and a little scared at the same time.

"Cause I'm getting a hard on."

But neither of us move. We just stand there, suddenly much closer than we realize, slapped in the face by our own fuckability—our bodies in their rawness, without the polish of a douche or antiperspirant. Hungry.

There is a pearl of wisdom taken from the worst decision I've made all night. It comes to me, written in blood and flashing through my brain as we stumble into the laundry room. As the leggings in question get pulled down. As the hard on in question gets pressed up against me. The answer.

You are supposed to smell this way.

Corners

The corners of my bed smell like different men I've invited to help me forget you, to mask your scent.

Bottom left, the artist whose name I forget. His large, rough hands that smelled like turpentine and clay.

The sheets between my legs, like that baby-faced bartender who left bite marks on my thighs, then kissed them back to bruise.

The bank teller, his blue shirt and bluer tie wrapped around my neck twice, pulled tight then flung to the bottom right; he fucked like we used to fight.

The bed lays twisted and unmade; I could wring out the sweat and bodies but wont. Let the odors seep into the mattress, let the stench permeate - anything to drive you out.

Last week, I fucked a guy because you share a name. I wanted to scream it over and over at the ceiling, rake it up and down his spine like I used to, yours. It was almost the same. I let him in twice and scratched you a letter bright red into his back.

I wake up naked, sheets stuck to my skin; always alone. I tug back a small tear into a fist-sized hole and look inside. It is space enough to bury my fist-sized heart. I consider it.

There was that college kid, *linguistics*, eager to *do it;* kept saying *do it*, only to stammer something thereafter about soccer and homework and Dustin Hoffman movies - his face flushed, panting, his pants still around his ankles; O! His mismatched socks! I bought him a six-pack and drove him to his dorm room.

Yesterday, I kissed a father of two and left him confused in a Walgreens parking lot after we *did it* in the back of his Saab. Fucking elsewhere seemed beside the point and I just wanted to go home.

For months I craved you. I mourned you in celibacy, as though it would make a difference. I wanted to smell you more than to kiss you. I wanted to burrow and coil up with you in silence; in the way animals speak with their bodies.

I made home, I nested; I waited and waited -

I don't love you anymore. I just want to feel mammalian again —

I almost did with a man who offered me breakfast; real slow, I let him lean into the soft and raw. We danced in the kitchen and he was gone by morning. Hating him reminded me of you.

Darling, I've fucked myself into a maze. All the aching corridors lead to your center.

What if I lit a funeral pyre on my sternum, fed it your head in my lap, dirty sheets, all my love and want and mistakes.

I fell asleep dreaming fire - your scent, burnt meat, the rain of ash muffling everything covering all trace. I dreamt and dreamt and dreamt I was dreaming, excited to show you my fist shaped heart, my new Saab, the black hole in my chest, healing. Me – your obedient beloved.

And I woke up. My body tucked into the crook of your arm, my face smashed against your armpit, and you still, so still in your sleep and breathing – our chests rising and falling as though we were again a singular organism.

We laid this way until I opened my eyes, *wanting.*

No, *hopeful.*

No, *foolish.*

Just morning

My two arms wrapped around body, the ache of floor.

The tender animal belly-up, pawing for touch - can you feel me?

Clutching fistfuls where you linger:

My skin, my hair, embedded

in all that flesh and softness -

Choking on memory, plastic bag, gasoline; on breaths full of you!

Only you – your scent in everyone, *everything*

Elegy

Am I no longer a useful instrument? A banjo, a sleeveless dress, a player piano - whichever suites you, whichever makes you love me best –

- makes your cold heart sing again. You, the bored composer, I the untouched keys - *Da Capo* return to me.

Kneeling on the bathroom floor, two hands holding my heart in place so that when I pitch forward in prayer, prostrate to my sorrow, it will not slip free or break -

No two instruments break alike: like songbird, like wolf cry. Imagine the cacophony of a heartbroken choir: a blue whale inside a cathedral, the clicks and moans reverberating stone through my bones into my disjoints and lonely -

My father married a woman named Mourning. My mother married a man named Loss. Your retreating form like my father's: the thud of the door, the drumming of these nervous fingers, percussive. My body left behind, the requiem my mother sings.

This is to say: blue notes are in my make; in the curve of my cello body, in its deep moan when pressed against you, your fingers moving across my neck, your thighs wrapped around mine, in your bow pulling, long and deliberate, across my chest –

We speak in minor key / metronome clipped.

My body remembers in movements: driving to work, awake at night, staring at not the wall but the space between myself and it where you used to sleep -

And In dreams I am your absence, a wild ceaseless crescendo, no apex. I hit the ceiling and double over, where I wake up, again, kneeling on the bathroom floor.

I am brass bells tolling your departure, parched lips moving over the wound, the accordion of ribcage swell and shrinking. I offer this useless instrument: my heart's gasping break - lungs sitting vigil, bloody organ, orchestral; the chipped keys, my conductor gone - *Da Capo al Fine*

Touch me please, I will sing you a song -

How else am I meant to love?

May Truth and the Lorde Set Me Free by Jeneé Darden

After the smoke cleared
I stood in the battlefield
Littered with broken, thorny stems
And crushed purple rose petals
On a ground saturated by
Violent tear shed
The smell of burning books
And my favorite skirt, stung my nostrils
Torn paintings stole my hope
Until I saw a bush of deep, purple roses across the way
And *Barefoot Dreams** held between the leaves
I walked toward the bush
Past the fallen soldiers I overpowered
I walked on the ground stained with their blood
My royal red carpet
Their amputated hands can't touch me anymore
I went to the rosebush
Kneeled down in the soil
Beholding my *Barefoot Dreams*
I saw the girl
Her white bows and plaited hair
Finally, visions of my womanhood are coming true
My, I've come a loooong way
From when...

They said Black girls from East Oakland are supposed to be tough. Daintiness is not an option. Feeling pain is not an option. They said my sensitivity was "on some white girl shit." And Black women don't have time to be depressed. Bright colors and pastels aren't an option on dark skin. Beauty is not an option for dark girls. "Stay your crow-colored ass out of the sun!"

But my darkness absorbs all that is light and warm. And the sun doesn't mind sharing with me.

I fought the world to embrace myself. I purged the poisonous messages in my brain that said my love for dresses, makeup and pretty things was wrong for girls like me. I purged poisonous messages that said women who look like me are never loved. Thank God Truth set me free. Sojourner Truth asked, " Ain't I a woman? Sista, ain't you a woman?" Well, HELL YEAH. I gave myself permission to be MY definition of woman. What an act of love. Truth cured me. Truth set me free.

I fought the world to embrace those warm feeling -- from my center. The ones that feel like flying comets traveling throughout every part of your body, and bursting into a glorious orange, light.

Sexual feelings weren't an option for me-- a Catholic schoolgirl, from a Baptist family. Liking boys wasn't an option.

"Baby girl, stick to the books and the Bible."

"Stay out of your flesh."

Thank God writers put naughty stuff in books. Thank God Black women write erotica and romance. I had to purge the poison again. Lorde delivered me. Audre Lorde said women have power in the erotic. I gave myself permission to bring passion and pleasure to all areas of my life, and connect spirit to my body. Lorde delivered me. Lorde delivered me from shameful feelings.

And God never stopped loving me.

* *Barefoot Dreams* is a painting by Brenda Joysmith

[soothing songs i weave for you] by Hannah Rubin

I spend every shabbat morning with my finger pressed deep into the page of my little red siddur, mouthing the words quietly as my brother sings my favorite prayer from the bima. Each lilt in his voice, the way the ends of certain words pick up and then drop, step by step— every sound its own ceremony. Tremors in the skin of my throat, a gentle massage, never loud enough for my mother next to me to hear. When she sings, it is all high high whisper voice warbling out of touch. I don't want to sing like her. I have rhythm. I keep my eyes trained real tight on the words. I let them inside.

The hebrew words are harsh and throaty to pronounce, wound up through the melody thick like honey. Together: a dissonance that sparkles. *Anim Zemirot* is all of my favorite things. Day of prayers, the torah with all its bells, wafting smells of a Kiddush waiting to be eaten. As my brother's mouth rounds the bottom of page 362, I imagine my little voice echoing daintily across the velvet blue carpet, everyone smiling. I know my cheeks would get all red and nervous, but I don't even care.

The Shul I go to has a confused identity, straddling the murky line between Conservative and Orthodox. There is no strict mechiza separating the men and women, but the seating is arranged in order to encourage you to do so on your own accord. People can drive to Shul, but only if they hide their cars a few streets away. Girls are allowed to run up on the bima to hide under the cantor's tallit at the end of services, but only if they are under a certain age. I can't exactly understand what that age is, and no one says it explicitly. It is just known. I am nearly too old now— but I still run up anyways. Because I love being covered in cloth, and getting to hide in front of everyone. A big secret.

Sometime in the early winter, I ask my dad if I can be the one to recite *Anim Zemirot* at services. He brushes it off, says something like, "oh you don't really want to do that." My teeth wrinkle because I'm certain he is wrong. I do want to. Some weeks go by and I remember and forget a bunch of times. And then, one day, while waiting in my Rabbi's office for a shiur to begin, I ask again. It seems as if everyone's heads look back and forth at each other, eyeballs going in different directions. Now, my whole town is here, circling around me, shifting their cheeks, hawk-like. A deep aura of discomfort ringing from my question, my desire. It is me and my Rabbi alone in the room, surrounded by his dark wooden furniture. "Let me think it over," he finally says, long white fingers resting on the table between us.

Eventually it is decided that, so long as it is before my Bat Mitzvah and my brother is standing there singing next to me—it is okay for me to sing *Anim Zemirot* for the congregation.

I am incredibly excited, a swooping wet feeling painted all across my insides. *Anim Zemirot!* I bug my brother constantly to practice with me—singing loud into his ears until he finally agrees.

Announcements will, of course, be made— in case anyone is too uncomfortable to attend.

I wonder sometimes, while I'm lying in the grass of my backyard and picking off pieces of bark from our dogwood tree, what happens at a Bat Mitzvah that would make it suddenly not okay for me to sing. My Bat Bitzvah feels a million years away, but in truth, it is probably quite soon. I hate Bat Mitzvah. The word even. I hate that my mom makes me wear a little piece of white cloth under my shirt because my nipples poke through the fabric if I don't. I hate that when I play Softball, my face gets all red and I smell just like my dad. I still remember the day my mom told me I couldn't walk around the house without a shirt on, even if I pulled my long hair down to cover over the pink spots on my chest. I still remember.

My brother and I do everything together as kids. I can't remember when we become different. But now he is chasing people on the ice skating rink in his black hockey skates, and I am in class on Sunday mornings twirling maniacally. He gets to wear his basketball jersey to class. He gets to sing.

My friends and I talk about boobs at lunch. Lara wants a DD cup. I'm skeptical. The white table cloth is ripped because my fingers are shredding it. *I feel like having boobs that big would just always get in the way.* I try to imagine running with those things flopping around and it hurts me. How will I play basketball with my dad on Saturday mornings? What if he accidentally touches them while I'm going up for a lay-up? Oh god. I am blushing deep at the table, and, we all agree, of course, that having big boobs is an experience that is worth it. How else will we be sexy? I fantasize most days about Hillel Abramson kissing me while we wait on the lunch line. I'm sure that will never happen if I don't have boobs. I think I want to be kissed more than I need to dribble some stupid basketball. We compromise: a C cup is the most ideal. And I can probably get them to stay down in one of those sports bra things.

I am told: wearing pants means you're less good than other people who don't wear pants, so wear a skirt, why don't you? My best friend Elisheva says she even wears skirts to sleep. I picture her brushing her teeth with a Scooby Doo sleeping shirt and her long black skirt. Her voice is nasal and her hair swishes past the middle of her back. She has seven sisters— three sets of bunkbeds spread across two rooms in a small house, and her mother wears a piece of black stretched across the back of her head so you can't see any of her hair. Her voice is nasal too. She also wears pearl earrings and has tan fingers and says nice things to me like *oh hannah, tell your mother i say hi.* I love when I get to go to their house and pull the basket of barbies out from under the bed. She bakes challah every week and lets me eat as much as I want. I don't tell Elisheva about singing *Anim Zemirot.* I don't think she will understand. When Tamara has a Spice Girls birthday party, she doesn't go. Says she doesn't like them because they wear those little shirts and sing too much.

That I have this ability to unintentionally provoke such discomfort in others, twists deep into me without my realizing it. Makes me profoundly uncomfortable with myself. The more I develop as a woman, the more thickly I feel it— somehow, something about me does something to other people, and I have to be careful about it. Even though I don't know what it is. I'm aware of this sometimes when my oldest brother throws things at me. Something about me makes him feel hatred. All I have to do is stand there.

It's purim, my favorite holiday! Last year I dressed up as a little chasidic boy and wore all of my brothers clothes! Everyone laughed! This year, I make my mom get me a poofy cinderella dress from a catalogue. I secretly want to be Jasmine but the mint green belly shirt scares me. The night of Purim, I put on my cinderella dress and dance around my room. My mom comes in to get me and I feel caught: my insides twisting, rapidly, until they are my outsides and my cheeks are brittle with discomfort. Everything is glittery and exposed— garish in the cheap lighting of my bedroom. Layers of sheer fabric like a loudspeaker saying *I am I am I am I am* and all of a sudden all the windows feel too cold. When we get to shul, I hide in the lobby, pressing my face to the glass doors, watching everyone inside the synagogue dance around the torah. I will not take my coat off.

The day that I get to stand on the bima and sing *Anim Zemirot* starts like any other. It is grey outside, I skip while walking to Shul, my dad holding his velvet tefillin bag on one side and my hand on the other. Once at Shul, I sit next to my mom in the second row with my feet dangling from the long wooden bench, with my hair in a tight bun. Throughout the whole service my heart is in my throat, choking me something awful. There aren't butterflies swooping through my chest— there are entire birds, with beaks and large bony wings, making a racket as they rebound around my insides. I am on edge, flipping back and forth between pages, singing the words manically in my head, afraid I will forget them. Heart bounding, breathless. I only have once chance. Maybe if I do a good enough job, they will forget I am a girl, and they will let me sing it again. And again. I so want to sing it again— not just twice even. Every week! Forever! I can wear my new satin blue suit and then my favorite purple dress with the big red flowers and afterwards during kiddush, everyone will come over to me and tell me how special I am, how good my singing was, how singing *Anim Zemirot* with me made them feel the best they ever were. No— that I am the best that there ever was. I want everyone to ring around me in a loopy circle, and I want everyone to tell me that they are so happy to know me.

When it comes time for *Anim Zemirot*, I walk up to the bima with my brother. I can tell he is embarrassed, cuz he has his hands in his pockets and his face is stuck in *that* look. The one he gets when we're at the dinner table eating *real people food* and all I want to eat are baked potatoes with melted cheese. We stand together, backs to the congregation, cream-colored pages of the prayer book in front of us. Blue velvet carpeting on the floor under my feet. We look at each other. Then we both look down. I open my mouth, a little cough comes out. He looks at me. We start again. Or, I try to start again. But no words come out. Everying is dry and throaty. Like the words are supposed to be, but instead, my whole esophagus has closed down. He is singing next to me. Every time I try to catch up, I have nothing to give. I stand there empty as his voice fills the room. He calls out his love for god. The congregation responds. *Anim Zmirot be'shirim e'erog. Ki elecha nafti ta'arog. Soothing songs and poems I weave, because my soul longs for you.* I stand there empty for the whole entire song. We walk back to our separate seats and the service continues.

I don't know if this story is an ending or a beginning.

I can still feel the way those words sound when you sing them the right way, they are like dancing little letters alighting on skin. I know that because I sang it so many times in front of the mirror to myself in my bedroom.

Nurses are supposed to save lives. They are the friendly, warm face liaising between doctor and patient. Nurses protect and preserve fragile existences, unless they are me on my birthday every ten years. I have to kill someone every decade on my birthday, or I will die.

My people are called Taricha. We look human, and for the most part, are just like humans. Like the taricha torosa, the California newt, we look harmless but are deadly.

I turned thirty-five at 2:37 this morning. I've agonized for the past week over whether I will take a life today or allow myself to fade away. I've barely slept. My hair desperately needs a relaxer, but I haven't had time or energy to go to the salon.

I've only had to do this once before, when I turned twenty-five. My first was an old man. He'd made it to ninety-six years old before cancer ravaged his body. He pleaded with me, with the doctors, even with the radiologist to let him go. He'd lived his life. He was as at peace with his mistakes as he was going to be. But when I pressed my hands against his chest, and his life slid up my arms and into my chest, I saw not peace but panic, disgust, regret in his eyes. Those eyes haunted me. I saw them each time I closed my own.

The eyes brought up guilt like bile into my mouth. But more than that, I became afraid of death. Seeing it first hand showed me the raw cruelty of it. I was with him, but I couldn't be *with* him. He went quickly, but it was as if time slowed down, extending his final brutal moments. Death was the ultimate bully, the abusive partner who separated you from anyone who could help, from all who could save, and painfully tore you away from all you love and who could love you. I knew from the second I saw the old man's eyes go blank that I would do it again, and again, to avoid feeling the way he felt.

And so, on my thirty-fifth birthday, I scoured the hospital searching for someone to kill. My patients were all in, obscenely, good health. I prayed for a gruesome trauma to enter the emergency room. I prayed for one of the other nurses to pass a dying patient on to me. I looked to pick up another shift. I needed to kill in a way that did not raise eyebrows or demand autopsies. My broken hip, inflamed appendix, bronchitis, and asthma attack were all easily treatable. My first shift ended without drama, and my second shift began without much hope. The emergency room was extraordinarily slow—sprained ankle, flu, concussion, broken finger. By ten at night, I was beginning to panic. I had until midnight.

Around 10:45pm, I began to pace the hospital in desperation and ended up in the emergency room again, praying for a grisly car accident. I tried to focus on charts, thinking that maybe if I stopped focusing on death, she would appear. Finally, at 11:30pm, I approached the young woman with the flu. She had a high fever and had passed out in the hospital bed with her chemistry flashcards resting on her chest. Her chest rose and fell quickly with ragged breaths, belabored by the mucus in her lungs. She was a college kid, first generation and premed. She did not budge when I checked her vitals. My hands trembled as they hovered over her chest. I pulled back, chastising myself for even thinking of taking the life of someone who had barely begun to live.

I went back to the nurse's station and tried to laugh with one of my coworkers about a drunk patient who would not stop singing Christmas carols even though it was April. But I knew my smile did not reach my eyes. My laughter felt fake. With a long sigh, I excused myself and went back to the girl with the flu.

When I reached her bedside, I saw the old man instead of her and my stomach turned. It was 11:58. I was running out of time. I couldn't remember my parents' last moments. I imagined it was slow, painful as Death snatched their breaths away. I turned back to the girl, forced myself to stop feeling, and pressed my hands against her chest. Her eyes and mouth snapped open. Her skin burned under my hands; her heart overheated and swelled. Sweat dripped from the tip of my nose onto her shirt. I closed my eyes to shut out her silent pleas. Her eyes, the smell of her hot skin, her youth would all plague me. But at least—at least—I would be alive.

Christine No is a writer, filmmaker and pitbull enthusiast based in Oakland, CA. She is a Pushcart Prize Nominee and the 2016 First Place Poetry Winner of the Litquake Writing Contest. Say hello at www.christineno.com

Gina Goldblatt is the founder of Liminal, a writing center for women, in Oakland California. She is a writer, an educator and an aerialist.

Hannah Rubin is a writer and artist based in Oakland, CA.

Heather Schubert is a published author, visual artist, teacher, Priestess and mother of four.

Jasmine Wade is obsessed with the tumultuous, hilarious, heartbreaking, and never-ending process of growing up. Find a list of her short stories at www.jasminehwade.com.

Jeneé Darden is an award-winning journalist, public speaker, mental health advocate and proud Oakland native. Visit her podcast and blog *CocoaFly.com* where she covers issues related to women, race, wellness and sex.

Norma Smith was born in Detroit, grew up in Fresno, California, and has lived and worked in Oakland since the late 1960s. In support of her writing, she has worked as a ward clerk in hospitals, as a radio producer, as a translator and interpreter, as an educator, and as an editor and writing coach.

Rebecca Gomez Farrell writes all the speculative fiction genres she can conjure up. Find a list of her published shorter works at RebeccaGomezFarrell.com, and find her debut fantasy novel, *Wings Unseen,* in August 2017 from Meerkat Press.

Ruth Crossman was born and raised in Berkeley and currently lives in Oakland. She is a poet and a songwriter who teaches ESL to support her writing habit.